LITTLE BOOK OF
BRITISH
GARDEN BIRDS

Liam McCann

LITTLE BOOK OF

BRITISH
GARDEN
BIRDS

First published in the UK in 2015

© Demand Media Limited 2016

www.demand-media.co.uk

Printed and bound in China

ISBN 978-1-911349-13-6

Contents

Introduction

A lmost three million of us have a passing interest in bird watching, whether that means keeping an eye on the bird table on the patio, scanning the skies with binoculars, building a hide in the forest or visiting one of many bird sanctuaries.

The serious 'twitchers' amongst us travel the length and breadth of the country in search of the rarest birds, while many of us are simply captivated by their flight and complex plumage. In Britain alone it is possible to see more than 400 species of bird.

This informative little book is a comprehensive guide to the birds you might find in your garden or near your home. It lists the key facts about each bird, their nesting and feeding habits, and when and where in the UK you can find them.

From the tiny Wren, Robin, Blue Tit, Goldcrest and Firecrest to scavengers like the Rook and Raven, and magnificent birds of prey like the Buzzard and Goshawk, each entry gives a fascinating insight into the lives of all the birds you are likely to glimpse in your garden or in the fields and forests across Britain.

A brief guide to bird populations in Britain:

Green:

The species that appear on the green list are not considered to be at risk.

Amber:

When a species' breeding population or range has declined by 25-50% in the last 25 years, has recovered from a historical decline, is a rare breeder, or is of either European or international importance, it is placed on the amber list of Birds of Conservation Concern.

Red:

When a species' breeding population has declined by more than 50% in the last 25 years, is not recovering from a historical decline, or is a globally threatened species, it is placed on the red list.

Barn Owl

Barn Owls are mainly nocturnal so they are seldom seen during the day, but they have a distinctive white heart-shaped face and dark eyes. Their feathers are mostly pale white but the female has more dark streaks on her back and breast than the male. She is also slightly larger.

The owls hunt over open farmland for small rodents such as mice and voles, but they will also eat frogs, small birds and insects. They usually hunt at night, using their exceptional sight to spot movement in the vegetation. When hunting during the day, they swoop low to the ground and occasionally hover before striking at smaller mammals.

The owls nest in trees, derelict buildings or in crevices on rocky escarpments or cliff faces. The female of the breeding pair incubates clutches of up to seven eggs throughout the summer. Both the adults will feed their young, but they will devote most attention to the oldest and biggest chicks if food is short. The youngest chicks may die as a result.

Barn Owl numbers have fallen dramatically – some conservationists estimate by 70% – across the UK in the last 30 years, primarily due to loss of habitat and decreasing numbers of prey animals. Their numbers have stabilised recently but they are still on the amber list.

Tyto alba

Length: **36cm**
Wingspan: **90cm**
Weight: **375g**
Breeding pairs: **5,000**
Present: **All year**
Status: **Amber**

Blackbird

The adult male Blackbird is easily recognizable with its glossy feathers, bright orange/yellow beak and distinctive eye ring. The female has medium brown plumage and a darker bill. The young have a slight red tint to their feathers that fades after the first moult. It's not unusual to find albino Blackbirds, and some have varying levels of pigment so they can be any colour from brilliant white to pure black.

Turdus merula

Length: **25cm**

Wingspan: **36cm**

Weight: **100g**

Breeding pairs: **4.4 million**

Present: **All year**

Status: **Green**

The adult's song varies wildly from mating calls to warnings, the former often rich like a flute and the latter accompanied by a chatter and flick of the wings. They often sing to themselves in the winter, but the song becomes more pronounced in the spring. From the end of the breeding season in July, the male won't sing until the following February.

The female builds a primitive nest in hedges or bushes from grass, twigs and mud, although they occasionally nest in sheds and outbuildings. As they are often low to the ground, the nests are frequently destroyed by cats, Magpies and birds of prey. The eggs are approximately an inch long and are incubated over 2-3 weeks. Both parents provide food once they've hatched.

The birds feed predominantly on insects and worms, but they have been known to eat snails, tadpoles and even small fish. They eat much more in the autumn and will often fight over fallen fruit. Many birds migrate south over the winter, but the overall UK population increases to around 20 million as more arrive from Northern Europe.

Blackcap

The Blackcap is a predominantly migratory bird from the warbler family that is a little smaller than a House Sparrow. The male has a black crown and forehead, greyish brown upper feathers and pale grey belly. The female's cap is reddish brown, and she also has browner upper parts and a buffer belly. The young are more like the female, but the males have a darker cap. They are all easily confused with the tit family and the Garden Warbler.

The birds feed on insects and bugs in the hedgerows and shrubs, but they are also known to eat berries during winter. They can occasionally be seen on bird tables.

The Blackcap's song begins with a chatter but then warbles into a sound like a flute. There are more similarities with the Garden Warbler but the Blackcap's song is usually shorter with longer pauses. The alarm call is a staccato click that sounds like stones being struck together.

The female builds the small nest in a hedge or bush, although they will occasionally use nooks and crannies in outbuildings. The breeding season begins in April and the female will usually produce two clutches of five eggs. The 17mm eggs only incubate for a maximum of two weeks and the hatchlings fledge for the same amount of time. As our winters get warmer, numbers remain higher as fewer birds migrate south to West Africa.

Sylvia atricapilla

Length: **13cm**
Wingspan: **22cm**
Weight: **20g**
Breeding pairs: **580,000**
Present: **Summer**
Status: **Green**

Blue Tit

The Blue Tit may have bright blue wings, tail and crown of its head, but it has a yellow belly, dark collar and eye stripe, and a white wing bar and cheeks. The female is roughly the same colour as the male but is usually slightly paler. The young are much duller in colour and start off largely green before the blue develops.

These tiny birds feed on insects, caterpillars, bugs, beetles and spiders, but they will also visit bird tables for seed or nuts. They used to peck

Cyanistes caeruleus

Length: **11cm**
Wingspan: **18cm**
Weight: **10g**
Breeding pairs: **3.3 million**
Present: **All year**
Status: **Green**

through the foil on top of milk bottles.

The female will make a tiny cup-shaped nest in holes in walls or trees, but they've also been found in letterboxes, gutters and open pipes.

It's rare for the female to have more than one clutch, so she lays 10-12 eggs instead. The eggs are usually white with dark spots. She will incubate the eggs for two weeks but both parents will feed the young, often with caterpillars. Blue Tits are territorial and will remain in close proximity to their place of birth for life.

Brambling

The Brambling is a member of the finch family. In the winter it resembles the Chaffinch with its black head and orange chest but its white tail distinguishes it from its cousin. The summer plumage is glossier and the blackness spreads further down the back. The orange also spreads round to the bird's back. The female plumage doesn't change as much but does become brighter in summer. The hatchlings are born brown and grey and are much more like the females.

Fringilla montifringilla

Length: **14cm**
Wingspan: **25cm**
Weight: **25g**
Breeding pairs: **Fewer than 10**
Present: **Winter**
Status: **Green**

The birds like to make a deep nest of moss, grass, feathers, wool and hair in conifer trees during the winter. The breeding season starts in May and the female lays up to nine eggs in one or two clutches. They incubate for around 11 days and fledge for a further two weeks. Both parents feed the chicks with a variety of seeds, berries and insects. They usually hunt for food in the trees but occasionally form flocks and graze along the ground. It may be rare in the UK but flocks of millions of birds are common where beech mast (nuts) grows.

Bullfinch

This muscular bird has a short dark bill, black wings, nape and crown, and a white rump. The male has a bluish back and pink breast, while the female is browner. The young resemble the female but don't have black crowns. The birds are generally shy and their soft song mirrors their nature, but the migratory birds that head to the UK from Northern Europe in the winter are bigger, louder and more confident.

The native females build a fragile nest of twigs and moss in hedgerows or bushes like blackthorn and hawthorn, but they can also be found in woodland or farmland. She lays up to three clutches of seven eggs from April onwards. They hatch after two weeks and are cared for by both parents. The birds usually eat berries, seeds and insects but they may take gardeners' buds and fruit and will also visit the bird feeder.

With their woodland habitats declining, they were on the endangered red list for much of the latter half of the 20th century but numbers have since stabilised.

Pyrrhula pyrrhula

Length: **15cm**

Wingspan: **25cm**

Weight: **32g**

Breeding pairs: **190,000**

Present: **All year**

Status: **Amber**

Buzzard

Buzzards typically have dark brown feathers with narrow bars across their paler chests and tails. The tail is short and broad, as are the wings, which are held in a V-shape when the birds soar looking for prey on the ground. They also appear hunched when perched as their necks are relatively short.

Buzzards eat mice, voles, rabbits and smaller birds, although they will also feed on insects, frogs, lizards and newts. They usually build a solid twig nest that's lined with moss or bracken in trees or on scrubland. They will often return to the same nest year after year.

The breeding season begins in spring and the female will lay one clutch of around four smooth eggs that are two inches long. They incubate for a month and fledge for nearly two months. The birds are more common in western Britain but they are slowly spreading east, and some even migrate to the east during the winter. They are also becoming more common in Ireland.

Buteo buteo

Length: **55cm**
Wingspan: **120cm**
Weight: **800g**
Breeding pairs: **14,500**
Present: **All year**
Status: **Green**

Carrion Crow

Carrion Crows initially appear black but their glossy feathers actually have a purplish-green iridescence. They are bigger than Jackdaws and smaller than Ravens, and closely resemble Rooks, although in flight their heads look shorter and their wings beat slower. Hooded Crows are more common in Ireland, but they have grey backs and bellies and are distinguishable by their black caps. They can often be confused with the juvenile Carrion Crow and the two races frequently interbreed.

Corvus corone

Length: **46cm**
Wingspan: **100cm**
Weight: **500g**
Breeding pairs: **800,000**
Present: **All year**
Status: **Green**

Crows nest in the forks of trees, on cliffs and even in unused chimneys. The nests are usually built with twigs and bark and can be quite large. The breeding season begins in late spring and the female will lay one clutch of around five eggs, which will incubated by the female only for nearly three weeks. Both parents feed the fledglings on a diet of insects, worms, fruit, human food waste, eggs and even small birds. They are often considered pests as they scavenge for the eggs of game birds. They can also terrorise Magpies and Wood Pigeons.

Chaffinch

The short and squat Chaffinch is extremely common in the UK. It has distinctive white bars on its wings, which are even brighter in the summer. The male has a pink chest and cheeks, bluish neck and a brown back. The female's back is a more olive brown, while her stomach is a little greyer and her rump turns from white to green.

The birds build a small cup-shaped nest from moss and feathers in the fork of a

Fringilla coelebs

Length: **15cm**
Wingspan: **25cm**
Weight: **25g**
Breeding pairs:
5.4 million
Present: **All year**
Status: **Green**

tree or in the middle of larger shrubs. The breeding season begins in April and the female will lay up to two clutches of eight eggs, each around 20mm long. The female alone incubates them for two weeks, and they fledge for an equal length of time. Both parents feed the chicks on seeds, caterpillars and small insects. The chicks rarely stray far from the nest throughout their lives.

The UK population increases by up to 20 million as migratory birds head south from Scandinavia during the winter.

Coal Tit

The tiny Coal Tit is the smallest European tit. A white patch on its nape distinguishes it from the Marsh Tit or Willow Tit. It also has olive-coloured upper feathers and a buff belly. Its crown and chest are much darker, but the cheeks and neck are white. Two white wings bars also help identify it. The young have browner upper feathers and yellowish cheeks, napes and wing bars.

Periparus ater

Length: **12cm**
Wingspan: **19cm**
Weight: **10g**
Breeding pairs: **610,000**
Present: **All year**
Status: **Green**

Coal Tits feed on seeds, beech mast and insects, but they will also take suet scraps from bird tables. They like to store food but they often forget where they've stashed seeds and their caches can be raided by other birds. The tits make a nest from wool, leaves and webs and line it with moss. Their tiny eggs are barely half an inch long, and the first hatchlings are usually born in May.

The birds are resident in the UK and rarely stray far from where they were born. Some continental birds join their flocks in the winter before continuing south.

Collared Dove

This dove gets its name from the distinctive black-and-white band around its neck, although young birds don't yet have the collar. The birds are smaller than Wood Pigeons and their colours are a much softer grey, which can have a pinkish or silvery tinge. In flight, its silhouette resembles a Sparrowhawk so other species give it a wide berth. Its call is a repetitive 'coo'.

Streptopelia decaocto

Length: **32cm**
Wingspan: **52cm**
Weight: **210g**
Breeding pairs: **300,000**
Present: **All year**
Status: **Green**

The birds build a fragile nest of twigs in a tree or on the ledge of a building. Breeding season begins in March and the female can lay up to five clutches of eggs. Both parents share the incubating role and the hatchlings are born two weeks later. They also share feeding duties, bringing their young a selection of grain, berries, caterpillars, aphids and insects. There were no breeding pairs in the UK 60 years ago, but they have gradually spread northwest across Europe and there are now around 300,000 pairs in Britain.

Common Gull

The colour of the Common Gull depends on its age and the time of year. In the summer, the adults are largely a bluish grey with a white head and chest. The legs and beak are yellow tinged with green and the wings have black tips. Their bills are a duller yellow and their heads are streaked with grey in the winter. Younger birds have much browner plumage. They are smaller than Herring Gulls but larger than Black-headed Gulls.

Both sexes build a nest from plant material, sometimes seaweed, usually as part of a colony. The breeding season begins in the early summer but the female will only lay one clutch of three eggs. Both parents will incubate the eggs for 3-4 weeks. They then provide the youngsters with a diet of carrion, worms, molluscs and small fish.

The British population increases 10-fold as Scandinavian birds join the resident population during the winter. Their overall numbers are in decline, however, most likely due to loss of habitat through land drainage and predation by mink.

Larus canus

Length: **41cm**
Wingspan: **110cm**
Weight: **400g**
Breeding pairs: **70,000**
Present: **All year**
Status: **Amber**

Coot

Coots are a charcoal-grey colour, although the forehead and bill are usually white. They also have a red garter midway up their legs. The birds are plump and resemble moorhens, although the young are much greyer and have a whitish face and chest. Coots build their nests using scavenged vegetation in shallow water. They feed on a mixture of duckweed, aquatic grass, snails and insect larvae, and they will occasionally take scraps from gardens.

Fulica atra

Length: **37cm**
Wingspan: **75cm**
Weight: **800g**
Breeding pairs: **46,000**
Present: **All year**
Status: **Green**

The breeding season begins in March and the female will lay 2-3 clutches of up to 15 two-inch eggs. Both parents incubate the eggs as they need constant protection from predatory fish, and the birds often fight over territory. As soon as the young hatch, the male takes them to the water.

Some Coots leave the UK in the winter but most remain and are joined by another 500,000 birds from Northern Europe. Overall, the population is increasing as gravel pits and reservoirs provide them with safer nesting grounds.

Crested Tit

Crested Tits are similar to the other members of the tit family but they are only found in small numbers in isolated forests in Scotland. Their large heads are off-white, and they have a black eye-line, ruff and collar. They have a unique speckled crest and whitish belly. As is so often the case, the juvenile birds are browner and lack the distinctive collar or pointed crest.

Female Crested Tits build a nest of moss and lichen in rotten

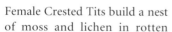

Lophophanes cristatus

Length: **12cm**
Wingspan: **18cm**
Weight: **11g**
Breeding pairs: **900**
Present: **All year**
Status: **Amber**

wood, but they will also use nest boxes. The breeding season begins in April but the female will only lay one clutch of around six eggs. She incubates them for two weeks but both parents will feed the hatchlings for three weeks during fledging. The young become independent within a month but they rarely stray far from where they were born.

They remain only in the Caledonian pine forests and are on the amber list as their numbers are still thought to be in decline. They occasionally form social groups with Coal Tits and Goldcrests and feed on insects, spiders and seeds.

Crossbill

Crossbills are more heavily built than the other members of the finch family. Females are a greenish grey with a yellow rump and dark wings. Males are usually a rusty red colour with darker wings and tails. The adults also have a forked tail and uneven mandibles, hence their name. Juveniles are a dull grey with streaked chests.

The female builds a cup-shaped nest in a conifer tree from twigs, grass and lichen. Breeding usually begins when the cone crops are plentiful in January but they have been known to mate from August until the following April. She will produce 2-10 eggs in two clutches, which she alone will incubate. The male will help with feeding when the chicks hatch two weeks later.

Their crossed bills allow them to eat larch, pine and spruce seeds but they will also feed on berries and small animals. They will follow the cone crop but, if it's poor or the weather is particularly cold, the birds will slow their metabolism and partially hibernate. More conifer forests have helped their numbers stay constant, although they are largely absent from the Midlands, Cornwall and central Ireland.

Loxia curvirostra

Length: **16cm**

Wingspan: **28cm**

Weight: **36g**

Breeding pairs: **10,000**

Present: **All year**

Status: **Green**

Cuckoo

The Cuckoo is another bird that can be mistaken for a Sparrowhawk when in flight. This confuses some birds, which often respond with a shrill alarm call before bolting. Adult males are blue-grey with white spots on the wingtips and tail. The females are the same colour, although they're sometimes born as rufous hepatic morphs with reddish pigment in the feathers. The young also have this red-brown tinge but this usually fades in adulthood. The male calls with the familiar cuckoo sound but the female tends to emit a bubbling chuckle.

These migratory birds arrive in Britain from central Africa in April and begin breeding at the end of May. Females may have as many as 25 clutches, each of a single egg. Cuckoos are brood parasites so the female lays her solitary egg in other birds' nests. As the chick is usually much larger than those of their Dunnock or Robin hosts, the Cuckoo chick ejects them from the nest so that it alone is raised by the host parents. Adult Cuckoos feed on beetles, ants and caterpillars that are poisonous to other species.

Cuckoos rely on healthy populations of host birds but, as Dunnock, Robin and Meadow Pipit numbers are in decline, so too are they and they are now on the red list.

Cuculus canorus

Length: **34cm**
Wingspan: **57cm**
Weight: **115g**
Breeding pairs: **30,000**
Present: **Summer**
Status: **Red**

Dunnock

The Dunnock is often mistaken for a Sparrow but it has a blue-grey chest, brown streaky back and pink legs. Its bill is narrower than the Sparrow's because it eats insects rather than seeds. The female doesn't have as much colour and the young have brown streaks on their heads and breasts. The adult's song is a soft warble that sounds like a cross between the Wren and the Robin.

Prunella modularis

Length: **15cm**
Wingspan: **20cm**
Weight: **20g**
Breeding pairs: **2 million**
Present: **All year**
Status: **Amber**

The female builds a nest from twigs and moss in hedgerows. The female incubates up to six eggs in three clutches, but both parents and any number of helpful males also bring food. This may be due to the fact that Dunnocks enjoy a varied sex life with multiple partners. The birds feed on beetles, spiders, seeds and berries.

The nests are often invaded by a single Cuckoo, which may oust the young from the nest and mimic their calls for food to confuse the host parents. This may have contributed to a fall in numbers during the 1980s, although some populations are now recovering.

Fieldfare

The Fieldfare is a large member of the thrush family that migrates south to Britain from Scandinavia before the harsh northern winter. Both sexes have a similar colour – bluish head, nape and rump with brown back and black tails – but the female is a little duller. The young have a brown head and are duller still.

Turdus pilaris

Length: **25cm**
Wingspan: **40cm**
Weight: **100g**
Breeding pairs:
Fewer than 10
Present: **Winter**
Status: **Red**

Very few Fieldfares breed in Britain as most of the 750,000 migratory birds head back north in the summer after the March-May breeding season. Those that do nest build a small cup of grass and moss that's lined with dirt. The female lays up to 15 eggs in two clutches and then incubates them for two weeks. They feed on fruit, worms, insects, spiders and snails.

Firecrest

The Firecrest is one of the smallest birds found in Britain. It is brighter than the Goldcrest and its green back, white belly, bronze collar and yellow stripe on the head are more vivid and sharper. The males have a bright orange crest, although this is much duller in the females and juveniles.

They feed on insects, springtails, spiders and moth eggs in woodland and are best seen in the autumn and win-

Regulus ignicapillus

Length: **9cm**
Wingspan: **12cm**
Weight: **5g**
Breeding pairs: **550**
Present: **All year**
Status: **Amber**

ter when larger numbers arrive from France and Spain. They breed in coniferous woodland after building compact triple-layered nests on branches. The female lays up to 12 eggs and incubates them alone, although both parents feed the chicks for a month after hatching. There can be competition for breeding territory with Goldcrests and other Firecrests but this usually amounts to aggressive wing-flapping and nothing more.

Garden Warbler

Warblers are stout birds with solid grey beaks and legs. They are a dull grey-brown colour with a slightly paler breast. Younger birds have an olive tint that gradually fades. They are shy birds that often hide in hedges before bursting into a beautiful song that mirrors that of the Blackcap. If startled, they issue a staccato alarm call. They migrate to the UK in the summer from

the savannahs of Sub-Saharan Africa. Their numbers fluctuate according to conditions and the availability of food to the south in the winter.

The Garden Warbler breeds almost anywhere there are trees, undergrowth and shrubs, particularly in woodland or large gardens. The male helps build a nest from dry grass and hair low to the ground in a bush. The female lays one or two clutches of up to seven eggs each in May and June, but the male will help incubating the eggs and then feeding the hatchlings.

Sylvia borin

Length: **14cm**
Wingspan: **21cm**
Weight: **19g**
Breeding pairs: **200,000**
Present: **Summer**
Status: **Green**

Goldcrest

The Goldcrest and Fire-crest are both smaller than the Wren – some weigh as little as a 20p piece – but the Goldcrest is much more abundant than its cousin as it has a broader habitat. The olive-green birds have whit-ish bellies and a distinctive gold stripe on the crown of the head. Younger birds are similar to their parents but they don't have the mark-ings on their heads until they reach breeding age. They communicate with a soft but high-pitched twitter.

Regulus regulus

Length: **9cm**
Wingspan: **14cm**
Weight: **6g**
Breeding pairs: **560,000**
Present: **All year**
Status: **Green**

The female builds the nest from moss, feathers and webs in the branches of conifer trees. The breeding season begins in late spring and the female will lay two clutches of around 10 half-inch eggs. Both parents will raise the chicks when they hatch, feeding them on spiders and small insects. Cold winters in the middle of the last century saw their numbers decline in the UK but the current period of warm weather has seen their numbers explode and there was almost an epidemic in 2005 when huge numbers arrived from Poland and Russia.

Goldfinch

This tiny finch has a red, white and black head, a golden body and yellow flashes on its wings. It also has white cheeks and splashes of red on its chin and forehead. Its chest is mostly white and the wings largely black. Males and females are almost indistinguishable except that

the female's face has fewer red feathers. Younger birds are a duller brown with dark streaks, and the head markings only develop later on.

The male attracts a mate with a sideways dance, colourful plumage and a delightful song. Breeding season begins at the end of April so the female builds a cup-shaped nest from moss and grass in a tree or dense shrub. She produces up to three clutches of seven half-inch eggs and incubates them alone, although the male will help with feeding once they've hatched. They tend to eat a restricted diet of seeds.

Many birds migrate in the winter but the same birds won't always head south year after year. Population numbers in the UK vary widely as a result, and they can also be boosted by an influx along the east coast from Northern Europe.

Carduelis carduelis

Length: **12cm**
Wingspan: **23cm**
Weight: **16g**
Breeding pairs: **220,000**
Present: **All year**
Status: **Green**

Goshawk

This powerful hawk with broad, blunt wings and tail is widespread in Wales, northern England and eastern Scotland, but largely absent from the rest of the UK, other than the odd isolated pocket. They look a little like Sparrowhawks and have brown wings and backs with a pale chest crossed with darker horizontal bars. Females are generally larger and browner, while juveniles are paler with greenish rather than yellow piercing eyes.

They feed on rabbits, squirrels and aquatic animals, plus large birds like Pheasants, Pigeons and Kestrels. They tend to ambush their prey but will also dive on mammals and smaller birds in the same way as Peregrine Falcons.

The breeding season begins in April but it is the male that builds the nest high in the trees. It is usually fabricated from twigs and bark and is often a bit of a mess. The female produces one clutch of up to five eggs, which she alone will incubate over the following five weeks. The male will provide food for the family but the female will take it from him and usually does the feeding. The young will eventually leave their birthplace but the parents are likely to remain.

Accipiter gentilis

Length: **55cm**
Wingspan: **125cm**
Weight: **1kg**
Breeding pairs: **400**
Present: **All year**
Status: **Green**

Great Tit

The Great Tit is similar in size to a House Sparrow and is the largest of the tit family. Males have a broader black stripe down their yellow chests than females but they are otherwise similar: black crown and throat; white cheeks, yellowish back; and blue-grey wings and rump. Their young are duller all over with yellow cheeks. They have a varied repertoire of song, of which the most recognisable sounds like

a bicycle pump and can be heard in spring and summer.

The breeding season begins in March and the female will lay up to two clutches of 15 eggs in an old nest or hole in a wall. The female incubates the eggs for two weeks, but both parents then feed the young on insects, spiders, berries and caterpillars. Adults will rarely stray far from their breeding grounds, although some will head for lower ground (and warmer temperatures) for the winter, where they are joined by large numbers of migratory birds.

Parus major

Length: **14cm**

Wingspan: **23cm**

Weight: **18g**

Breeding pairs: **1.6 million**

Present: **All year**

Status: **Green**

Greenfinch

The Greenfinch is a robust olive green bird with yellow wing surrounds and grey cheeks. It also has a forked tail. The female has fewer yellow flashes and has grey-brown breast feathers. Their young are more like the female but have darker streaks and are often mistaken for Sparrows.

The female builds a nest of twigs and grass in

Carduelis chloris

Length: **15cm**
Wingspan: **26cm**
Weight: **29g**
Breeding pairs: **550,000**
Present: **All year**
Status: **Green**

hedges and shrubs. Breeding begins in April and she will lay 2-3 clutches of up to eight eggs. She incubates them for two weeks, but both parents will then provide food, which usually consists of berries, buds and seeds. The young fledge for another fortnight but then leave the nest and frequently head to the continent for the winter.

A decline in hedgerows and changes in farming have forced Greenfinches to nest elsewhere but they have adapted well and their numbers are strong.

Green Woodpecker

The Green Woodpecker is the largest native member of the family in the UK. It has a red crown and neck, black around the eye, whitish belly, and green wings. The male has a distinctive red flash to his moustache, and juveniles have more black speckles on their underparts. The woodpecker uses its powerful tail for stability, and its feet have two rear-facing toes for extra grip.

The birds build a nest in a hole in a tree in April. The female lays one or two clutches of around six eggs, which are then incubated by both parents. They also share the feeding duties and will bring a variety of insects, beetles, caterpillars and ants back to the nest. The young will fledge for nearly a month and will finally leave the nest in the autumn. Their parents will remain at the nesting site. These sites have come under threat in the last 20 years and the species is now on the amber list.

Picus viridis
Length: **32cm**
Wingspan: **41cm**
Weight: **200g**
Breeding pairs: **15,000**
Present: **All year**
Status: **Amber**

Grey Heron

Grey Herons have white heads, necks and bellies. They also have a black crest and throat. The inner half of their wings are grey, while the outer half are much darker. Their young are darker still and are missing the long crest plumage.

Adults tend to alight near water and retract their necks to give a hunched appearance. There they wait to strike at fish, although they will also eat frogs, lizards, newts, mice, voles and occasionally small birds. They can empty ponds of fish in no time so they are often seen as a pest, but hunting them has become illegal and their numbers are slowly increasing.

They nest in trees in February and the female produces a couple of clutches of up to seven eggs that can be two inches long. Both adults build the nest and they then share feeding duties. They tend to stay near their nesting colonies but some migrate to Northern France in the winter.

Ardea cinerea

Length: **95cm**
Wingspan: **185cm**
Weight: **1.75kg**
Breeding pairs: **13,000**
Present: **All year**
Status: **Green**

Grey Partridge

The Grey Partridge is smaller than a Pheasant but larger than a Quail. They have a rather dull grey colour but this is interspersed with streaks of brown, their tails are brick red and their chests are a vivid orange. Males have a horseshoe mark on their bellies but this is not as noticeable in the females. Their young are mostly brown and lack the distinctive markings.

The breeding season begins in April and both parents build a sheltered nest on the ground to conceal it from predators. The hen lays a single clutch of up to 20 eggs.

Perdix perdix

Length: **30cm**
Wingspan: **46cm**
Weight: **400g**
Breeding pairs: **150,000**
Present: **All year**
Status: **Red**

The male doesn't help with incubation duties but he will share with feeding. Adults eat mainly seeds and grain but the chicks will feed on insects. The young don't develop wing feathers for a few days but they are fully fledged after a month or so. The entire family is likely to stay near the breeding ground, even though the use of pesticides and destruction of their habitat has led to a rapid decrease in their numbers. They are often bred on estates and shot for sport, but their numbers here are well managed so their long-term future could be assured.

Grey Wagtail

The Grey Wagtail uses its tail for stability in flight, which it wags constantly as it tries to catch insects. It has a bright yellow chest, black wings and a blue-grey back. The female has a paler breast and a lighter throat, which is similar to the male's winter coat. Juveniles closely resemble the females. They sing with a delightful trill and call with a staccato 'chic'.

The breeding season begins in late spring and both sexes

Motacilla cinerea

Length: **19cm**
Wingspan: **26cm**
Weight: **19g**
Breeding pairs: **34,000**
Present: **All year**
Status: **Amber**

build a nest from twigs and grass near to water. The female lays up to two clutches of seven eggs and incubates them herself. The male helps feed the hatchlings with tadpoles, water snails and midges that also live alongside water. Two weeks later, the young are able to fly, although they rarely migrate and usually don't stray too far from their birthplace. They occasionally find themselves in cities but only if there's a good water supply.

Hawfinch

Hawfinches are heavyset and powerful with a conical bill, brick-red back, buff belly and orange-brown head. In complete contrast, the wings are a dark and glossy blue with a white patch. Their bills are a faded blue in the summer and yellow in the winter. Their young have more of an orange tint to the head and a grey to the belly with dark spots.

The birds have incredibly powerful beaks and can crush cherry stones to reach the seeds. They also feed on buds, insects, beetles and more seeds. Both parents build a fragile nest in a tree in April and the female produces a maximum of

Coccothraustes coccothraustes

Length: **18cm**
Wingspan: **31cm**
Weight: **55g**
Breeding pairs: **5,000**
Present: **All year**
Status: **Red**

two clutches of seven eggs. She will incubate them for up to two weeks, and both parents will feed the young for another two weeks until they're ready to fly. The UK population booms with the arrival of migratory birds from Northern Europe in the winter, but the resident population rarely leaves these shores for warmer climes.

House Martin

These summer visitors have glossy dark backs and wings, and white underparts. Their forked tails have a brown tint and they also have a splash of white feathers around their feet. They have forked tails but are missing the streamers associated with Swallows. Their young have brown heads and grey chests. Adults appear black and white when flying, so they are easily confused with Swifts or Sand Martins. They tweet all summer and issue a soft chirrup as a call.

Delichon urbicum

Length: **13cm**
Wingspan: **27cm**
Weight: **18g**
Breeding pairs: **375,000**
Present: **Summer**
Status: **Amber**

Breeding begins in April and both parents build a muddy nest in a colony, often under the eaves of older houses. They and their offspring will return to the same nesting site year after year. The female lays a couple of clutches of around four eggs, but both parents will share incubation and feeding duties. Monitoring a migratory population isn't easy but it's thought that their numbers are declining. They spend the winter in central Africa.

House Sparrow

There may be nearly four million breeding pairs in the UK, but the House Sparrow population is in sharp decline and the birds have disappeared from many parts of Britain. Males have brown backs with black streaks, grey heads and chest, and a faded white wing bar and cheeks. The size of their black bib determines their standing in the flock. Females are

paler but have a yellowish stripe next to the eye. The young are very similar to their mothers.

Breeding begins in May, with both parents manufacturing an untidy nest of rubbish and other detritus close to human populations. The female lays three clutches of up to five eggs, which are then incubated by both parents. The male also helps with feeding, bringing the youngsters insects, seeds, berries, nuts and kitchen scraps.

The young fledge for a couple of weeks but will stay near their birthplace for life. In late summer, they occasionally scout nearby farmland for grain. Their numbers are in sharp decline but the cause remains unknown. Several theories have emerged from predation by cats, loss of habitat, competition with Collared Doves and a decline in the insect population due to pollution.

Passer domesticus

Length: **15cm**
Wingspan: **23cm**
Weight: **28g**
Breeding pairs: **3.6 million**
Present: **All year**
Status: **Red**

Jackdaw

The Jackdaw is the smallest of the crow family and, like the Rook or Carrion Crow, it is a highly intelligent and inquisitive animal. Adults are predominantly black, although they have a grey neck and shoulders and whitish eyes. The young are very similar but their eyes are often pale blue and they have a darker nape. As it is closer in size to a Jay or Pigeon, its flight is more hurried than the Rook or Raven.

The birds breed in colonies in April and often take over unused nests of larger birds. They then add twigs, hair and bark, and the female eventually lays a single clutch of five eggs. She incubates the eggs but both parents will feed the young a varied diet of insects, seeds, worms, fruit, berries and scraps. The adults will also eat rodents, mice and voles.

The birds often migrate to the lowlands during winter, and numbers are boosted by an influx from Northern Europe in the autumn. Their population is increasing slightly as Jackdaws will eat almost anything.

Corvus monedula

Length: **33cm**
Wingspan: **70cm**
Weight: **250g**
Breeding pairs: **400,000**
Present: **All year**
Status: **Green**

Jay

The Jay is a member of the crow family but it has much more colour: pale pink underparts, black-and-white flecked head, white throat and rump, black wings and tail, and blue eyes. It also has blue-and-white patches on the wings. Jays are sociable birds and often raise their crests before calling in a variety of styles, some that mimic other crows.

Jays begin to breed at the end of April and both parents

Garrulus glandarius

Length: **35cm**
Wingspan: **55cm**
Weight: **170g**
Breeding pairs:
150,000
Present: **All year**
Status: **Green**

build an untidy nest in a tree or shrub. They will then mate for life. The female incubates her clutch of up to 10 eggs for just over two weeks, but the male will help feeding the young. They fledge for another three weeks but will rarely stray far from their nesting grounds.

Adults often scavenge for other birds' eggs but they will also feed on acorns, fruit, insects, bats and young birds. This makes them unpopular with humans and they are often shot by fishermen who use their feathers for lures.

Kestrel

Kestrels are small brown birds of prey with hooked bills and black wingtips that can often be seen hovering above fields waiting to strike at small mammals on the ground. The male has a spotted chest and a hint of blue in the head and tail. The female is darker and her feathers are crossed with black bars. She has a cream chest and her head and tail might contain grey. The young closely resemble their mothers.

Kestrels breed from April onwards and like to nest on cliffs or buildings with high ledges. Both parents will add sticks and grass to complete the nest, and the female will lay up to nine eggs in a single clutch. She will incubate them for a month and then feed them food brought back to the nest by the male. The adults prefer shrews, mice, Starlings, beetles and grasshoppers. They can also see in ultraviolet, which is handy for hunting voles as their urine reflects UV light. A decline in the mammalian population on farmland has led to fewer Kestrels surviving the winter.

Most populations are resident, although some will migrate to the southern lowlands in winter. Youngsters will eventually leave the nest and travel up to 100 miles from their birthplace.

Falco tinnunculus

Length: **30cm**
Wingspan: **62cm**
Weight: **170g**
Breeding pairs: **50,000**
Present: **All year**
Status: **Amber**

Kingfisher

Kingfishers are small and stout with long bills, short tails and striking two-tone plumage: electric blue backs and tails with bright orange cheeks and chest. They have white flashes on the throat and collar. Females can be distinguished by the red mark on the lower half of their bills. Juveniles have the same markings but their colours are duller.

The birds breed from late April. Both sexes build a nest by excavating a tunnel on a riverbank. The female lays up to three clutches of seven eggs, which are then incubated by both sexes. The male also helps to rear the young when they hatch after three weeks. Kingfishers feed on freshwater fish but will also eat molluscs, amphibians and insects. They perch over the water and strike directly from above. The fish are taken back to the branch, stunned and swallowed headfirst.

The birds are mostly resident in the UK and the young rarely travel far from their place of birth. Their numbers have increased since Britain's rivers have become less polluted, but they are still considered at risk.

Alcedo atthis

Length: **16cm**
Wingspan: **25cm**
Weight: **37g**
Breeding pairs: **6,000**
Present: **All year**
Status: **Amber**

Lapwing

The Lapwing is about the size of a Pigeon and is one of the UK's larger wading birds. Its lower feathers appear white but they are actually a sparkling mix of green and purple, and only the cheeks and breast are white. Its back and wings are much darker, like its throat in summer. Females have a shorter crest, whiter breast and darker face. They are extremely aerobatic and will perform stunts to attract a mate in spring.

Vanellus vanellus

Length: **29cm**
Wingspan: **73cm**
Weight: **225g**
Breeding pairs: **100,000**
Present: **All year**
Status: **Red**

Breeding starts in March when the female builds a shallow nest on open ground. Both parents will incubate a single clutch of 3-4 eggs, and they continue to care for the chicks when they are born a month later. Young Lapwings are soon capable of fending for themselves but they will fledge for another month. Most birds are resident in the UK but some will migrate to Ireland while others head for France and Spain. In the winter, up to two million migratory birds arrive in the UK from Northern Europe.

Lesser Spotted Woodpecker

This small woodpecker has a black-and-white head, cheeks and throat; black back, wings and tail; and a whitish chest. The male has a red crown while the female's is white. Their young may have a dash of red like their father and some have browner bellies with streaks. They use their sturdy tails for support when tapping at trees, and two of their toes face backwards, giving them extra grip on vertical surfaces. The male drums his beak and issues a weak call not dissimilar to that of a Kestrel.

Breeding season begins in April and both sexes excavate a hole in a tree to use as a nest. The female lays one clutch of 3-8 eggs but the male helps incubate them over the next two weeks. Both parents then feed the young on insects, larvae, nuts and berries. They will only travel more than a few miles from the nest when food is scarce in winter as they are resident in the UK and don't migrate. Competition with other species, rotten trees being removed, and diseases like Dutch Elm have had a negative impact on their numbers and they are still declining.

Dendrocopos minor

Length: **15cm**
Wingspan: **26cm**
Weight: **20g**
Breeding pairs: **2,500**
Present: **All year**
Status: **Red**

Linnet

The Linnet has the characteristic forked tail of the finch family. Its feathers are mostly chestnut with a streaked whitish belly. The male dons a distinctive red forehead and bib in the summer but this fades at the onset of winter. Their young are more like the female but their feathers are even paler, although they often have more obvious streaks. The adult call is a fast-paced twitter, while the song is a breathless warble.

Carduelis cannabina

Length: **14cm**
Wingspan: **23cm**
Weight: **17g**
Breeding pairs: **500,000**
Present: **All year**
Status: **Red**

The birds breed in April so the female builds a small grassy nest lined with wool. She lays a couple of clutches of a handful of eggs and incubates them herself. Both parents feed the young a variety of insects and seeds. Their numbers have declined sharply in the last 40 years due to different farming practices and the use of herbicides.

Little Owl

The Little Owl has grey-brown upperparts wings and head, although it does have white speckles and its belly is much paler. It has yellow eyes and white eyebrows, while the legs and feet are both covered with feathers. The female is generally larger than the male with a similar colouring. Their young don't have as many speckles and the browns are duller.

Athene noctua

Length: **22cm**
Wingspan: **56cm**
Weight: **180g**
Breeding pairs: **12,000**
Present: **All year**
Status: **Green**

They are often seen in the day, and they give a distinctive bob of the head when trying to judge distances to prey or people. Both sexes call during the April mating season, and the male also whoops. Both sexes build a nest in a hole in a tree, in a crevice or in hedgerows and parks. The female lays a couple of clutches of around four eggs and incubates them herself for a month. Both parents feed the chicks while they fledge for the next five weeks.

Little Owls may be decreasing in number across the continent but their population is stable in the UK.

Long-tailed Tit

This tit is actually a member of the Aegithalidae family. It is a tiny pink bird with a white crown streaked with black. They have a very small bill, red eye rings and a long black-and-white tail. Females are similar to males but the juveniles don't have the distinctive pink breast.

The breeding season begins in April and the female takes up to three weeks to build a nest of moss, lichen and feathers. She incubates one

Aegithalos caudatus

Length: **15cm**

Wingspan: **18cm**

Weight: **8g**

Breeding pairs: **210,000**

Present: **All year**

Status: **Green**

or two clutches of up to 16 eggs, but her partner and other males that have failed to mate will all help raise the chicks.

The birds rarely move far from their nesting grounds, although they can join up into small flocks to look for food in the winter. If it's particularly cold, they will huddle together to share bodily warmth. As our winters become milder, their population has increased and the species is thriving.

Magpie

Magpies are predominantly black and white but their feathers do glow with a glossy green and purple iridescence. Their tails can sometimes be more than half the length of their body, which can indicate how dominant the bird is in its social group. **Young birds have shorter tails and faded white underparts, and their black upper feathers are also duller.**

They gather at breeding time in early April but usually spend time establishing a pecking order and resolving conflicts before pairing off. Both parents build a complex nest of twigs and vegetation in trees or on buildings or pylons. They sometimes add a domed roof to protect their chicks from predators. The female lays one clutch of around six eggs and incubates them alone, although both parents provide food and feed the chicks. They eat insects, eggs, other chicks and rodents, but may also feed on berries and fruit. The birds used to be perceived as mischievous, cannibalistic and unlucky so they were often shot, but their numbers have now increased.

Pica pica

Length: **45cm**
Wingspan: **55cm**
Weight: **225g**
Breeding pairs: **600,000**
Present: **All year**
Status: **Green**

Marsh Tit

It's difficult to tell the Marsh Tit and Willow Tit apart, but the Marsh Tit has more defined lines, a smaller bib and a darker black cap. Its cheeks are white and its neck is short, and it also lacks the distinctive pale wing patch of the Willow Tit. It either has a square tail or a slight fork, and its upper feathers are sandy brown. The young have a duller black cap.

Poecile palustris

Length: **12cm**
Wingspan: **18cm**
Weight: **11g**
Breeding pairs: **60,000**
Present: **All year**
Status: **Red**

The breeding season begins in April so the female builds a moss-lined nest in a hole in a deciduous tree. She lays up to two clutches of 11 eggs and incubates them alone, although the male will help feed the chicks with sunflower seeds, insects and small garden scraps.

The young rarely stray far from their birthplace, but changes in woodland management have seen their numbers decline recently.

Mistle Thrush

This thrush is bigger and lighter than the Song Thrush. Its pale breast and flanks are heavily spotted and the wings have pale edges. The underside of the wings are white, which can clearly be seen as it flies – it tends to flap powerfully a few times and then glide for a distance. The young are paler and have more spots on their backs and necks. They tend to sing in stormy weather, and

their calls sound like the clack or chatter of a football rattle.

Turdus viscivorus

Length: **27cm**
Wingspan: **45cm**
Weight: **125g**
Breeding pairs: **220,000**
Present: **All year**
Status: **Amber**

Breeding starts at the end of the winter and runs into May. The female alone builds a grassy nest in the fork of a tree or in a hole in a wall. She lays two clutches of around five eggs and incubates them by herself for two weeks. The male will provide worms, slugs and berries for them to feed on. The birds are largely resident in the UK, although some will migrate to Ireland or Northern France in winter.

Nightingale

Nightingales are shy birds that can often be glimpsed hiding in dense shrubs. The birds have a plain brown chest with a reddish-brown rear. Their underparts are paler, and they have a black eye with a white surround. Their young can be confused with juvenile Robins, both in looks and in their delicate song but the Nightingale's is more powerful, rich and melodious.

Luscinia megarhynchos

Length: **14cm**
Wingspan: **21cm**
Weight: **19g**
Breeding pairs: **5,500**
Present: **Summer**
Status: **Amber**

The birds breed from mid-May into the summer, and it is the female alone who builds a grassy nest on the ground among the leaves. She will also incubate her single clutch of around four eggs alone, although the male will provide insects and berries for sustenance. The birds are migratory and only come to the UK to breed in the summer. They arrive in southern England in April and leave for central Africa in September. Colder and wetter springs have restricted their breeding range so they are becoming rarer in England.

Nuthatch

The Nuthatch has yellowish legs, an orange chest and blue-grey back, wings, crown and nape. It also has a black eye stripe across its white cheeks so it looks like a highwayman. Their young look very similar to the adults but they are duller in colour. The birds have a long bill and short tail, and they climb using their powerful feet.

Sitta europaea

Length: **15cm**
Wingspan: **22cm**
Weight: **22g**
Breeding pairs: **140,000**
Present: **All year**
Status: **Green**

The breeding season begins at the end of spring. The female will either rebuild an old nest and plaster it with mud for strength or find a hole in a wall and add bark for stability. They will also use nest boxes. The female lays a couple of clutches of up to 13 eggs and incubates them alone for two weeks. The male will help provide a diet of nuts and seeds, although they tend to catch insects and beetles in the summer.

The young fledge for 3-4 weeks and most will stay close to their birthplace. They have spread north into Scotland as the climate warms and their numbers are very strong across the UK.

Peregrine Falcon

The female falcon is larger than the male but they are similar in appearance: they have long, pointed wings; a short tail; grey underparts with a paler breast; a whitish face with darker moustache; dark wings; and dark bands on the tail. They are powerfully built and are known for catching other birds in a stooping dive that can reach speeds of up to 180mph. Juveniles are slightly greyer and have dark brown streaks on their chests.

The spectacular dive is used to kill or incapacitate game birds in flight. The falcon strikes with its talons and then delivers a fatal bite to the back of the neck. As they used to kill racing pigeons, they themselves were hunted but their numbers have now recovered.

The breeding season begins in March and the female will lay around four eggs in a nest on a cliff face or tall building. The male occasionally helps with incubating the eggs in the four weeks before they hatch. The young fledge for another 5-6 weeks, and they will remain close to their birthplace having left the nest.

Falco peregrinus

Length: **45cm**
Wingspan: **105cm**
Weight: **675g**
Breeding pairs: **1,500**
Present: **All year**
Status: **Green**

Pheasant

Pheasants were brought into the UK as a game bird by the Normans after the Battle of Hastings. Males have a bright copper chest, purple throats, green flashes on the head and brown speckles on their backs and tails. The female is dull by comparison and is beige with brown streaks. Their young are more like the female but they have shorter tails.

Phasianus colchicus

Length: **83cm**
Wingspan: **85cm**
Weight: **1.2kg**
Breeding pairs:
1.5 million
Present: **All year**
Status: **Green**

The breeding season begins in April and the female will build a shallow nest on the ground in long grass. Males may have more than one mate and will fiercely defend their territory from rivals trying to woo their hens. The female will lay one clutch of up to 15 eggs and incubates them alone but some won't survive as the nests are vulnerable to predators. Pheasants are protected game birds so their numbers are stable, and they are found across the whole of the UK other than a corner of northwest Scotland.

Pied Flycatcher

The small males have black backs and wings and white underparts. Their tails have white edges and they have a white patch on their wings. They also have a tiny white speck on their foreheads. Females are mostly brown and a duller white, much like their young, although they also have speckled bellies.

These migratory birds arrive in the north and west of the UK in April and it is the female who claims a territory.

Ficedula hypoleuca

Length: **13cm**
Wingspan: **22cm**
Weight: **12g**
Breeding pairs: **35,000**
Present: **Summer**
Status: **Amber**

They breed from May when she builds a nest from leaves, grass and hair in a hole in a tree in a garden, park or woodland. She will incubate one clutch of around five eggs for two weeks, although the male will help feed the hatchlings with insects, flies, woodlice, beetles and ants. When food is scarce, they will eat seeds and fruit. They head back to western Africa in August and won't return to the UK for nine months.

Pied Wagtail

This small black-and-white bird is sometimes mistaken for a juvenile Magpie, although it is actually much smaller and is easily distinguishable by its constantly wagging tail. In summer, the male has a white forehead and belly, and black crown, neck, flanks and wings. His winter plumage is much greyer, which is similar to the female. Their young are mostly brown but may have a yellow tint.

Motacilla alba yarrellii

Length: **18cm**
Wingspan: **27cm**
Weight: **24g**
Breeding pairs: **300,000**
Present: **All year**
Status: **Green**

The birds breed in May and nest in buildings or the disused nests of other birds. The female lays one or two clutches of up to seven eggs and both parents incubate them for two weeks. They also take turns feeding the hatchlings on insects and caterpillars. The birds tend to stay near their birthplace but some migrate across the English Channel in winter. Their numbers are generally stable in the UK but some populations have declined along waterways.

Raven

Ravens are the largest crows found in the UK. They appear hunched because their necks are short and covered with bushy feathers. Their feathers seem jet black but they have a glossy purple sheen. Their bills are thick and powerful, their eyes small and dark. The young are a little browner and their eyes are paler. When trying to attract a mate in spring, they will perform astonishing aerobatics.

Corvus corax

Length: **65cm**
Wingspan: **135cm**
Weight: **1.2kg**
Breeding pairs: **7,000**
Present: **All year**
Status: **Green**

The breeding season starts in the winter and the birds nest in the uplands as well as on the coast. The female lays one clutch of 4-6 eggs on a ledge or in the fork of a tree. Both parents build the nest but the female alone will incubate the eggs for three weeks. The male will supply a selection of carrion, small mammals, birds and insects on which to feed. The chicks often stay in the nest for several months before dispersing and finding their own territory. Scottish populations are declining sharply, although numbers further south are slowly increasing.

Redwing

Redwings migrate to the UK from Scandinavia and Iceland to avoid the harsh Arctic winters. They have pale breasts with browner upperparts and reddish flanks. They also have a noticeable yellow or white stripe above the eyes. Juveniles have paler spots on their backs.

The birds breed from April onwards and build a small nest of twigs

Turdus iliacus

Length: **21cm**

Wingspan: **34cm**

Weight: **65g**

Breeding pairs: **Fewer than 60**

Present: **Winter**

Status: **Red**

and grass in a tree or bush. The female incubates a couple of clutches of around five eggs but both parents will feed the chicks when they hatch two weeks later. They eat worms, snails, slugs and insects, as well as berries and fruit. There are so few breeding pairs in the UK that Redwings are red listed as a conservation concern.

Robin

Robins are easily distinguished by the their plump appearance, bright orange breast and face, brown wings and white belly. Adult males and females are very similar but their young have brown speckled wings and chests. These feathers are lost when the birds are a couple of months old and only then do the familiar red feathers come through. They are very shy in the summer and rarely sing, but they are abundant in winter and their song becomes much more noticeable.

The breeding season begins in March and they tend to make a nest of grass and leaves in a tree stump or hole in a wall. The female lays 2-3 clutches of around six eggs and she alone will incubate them for two weeks. The male will help rear the chicks, feeding them insects, worms and sunflower hearts.

Native Robins rarely migrate, although some will head south to Spain for the winter. Scandinavian birds arrive at around the same time. They will fight for territory, sometimes to the death, and will also terrorise the tit family and Dunnocks in the battle for food. Their numbers are strong and stable, although they can be hit by especially cold winters.

Erithacus rubecula

Length: **14cm**
Wingspan: **21cm**
Weight: **19g**
Breeding pairs:
4.2 million
Present: **All year**
Status: **Green**

Rook

Rooks look a little dishevelled with their ragged thigh feathers and shaggy peak. They are all black but their feathers sometimes glow with a red or purple gloss. Adults have a patch of bare skin around the base of the powerful bill, but juveniles don't so they can be confused with the Carrion Crow. Rooks nest in colonies and often flock together, whereas Carrion Crows are more solitary.

Corvus frugilegus

Length: **45cm**
Wingspan: **85cm**
Weight: **500g**
Breeding pairs: **860,000**
Present: **All year**
Status: **Green**

They breed from March in nests high in the trees. The nests are so sturdy that they may be used year after year with minor renovations. The female lays a single clutch of up to nine eggs and incubates them herself, although the male will help with feeding duties. They eat a variety of insects, carrion, fruit and seeds. The young will fly the nest and can travel great distances but the parents are largely sedentary. The native UK population is boosted by the arrival of European migrants in winter.

Siskin

This is a small and agile member of the finch family. They are a mix of yellow, green and brown but have a darker belly, forked tail and brighter yellow flash on the rump. Males have a darker head and brighter cheeks, while the female has more streaking. Juveniles are browner still and have even more streaks.

The breeding season starts in the middle of spring so

Carduelis spinus

Length: **12cm**
Wingspan: **21cm**
Weight: **15g**
Breeding pairs: **300,000**
Present: **All year**
Status: **Green**

the female builds a small nest in a conifer tree. She incubates two clutches of around four eggs for two weeks, but the male will help to feed the young on cone seeds. They will also venture into gardens to take peanuts from feeders.

Siskins remain near their birthplace except when food runs short, in which case they head south. Many birds arrive from the continent to spend the winter in the UK. Numbers are reasonably stable but they may be declining gradually in some areas.

Song Thrush

Both sexes have a deep brown back and wings, paler chest and dark brown speckles. They have a tuft of pure white on the belly and a brown bill. Their young have paler streaks along their backs. They have a crisp song that repeats several times and sounds like a flute.

The birds breed in March and the female builds a nest in a sheltered spot in a tree or shrub. She lays several clutches of around seven eggs into early summer. She alone incubates them but the male will provide food. They eat worms, berries and insects, but they will also feed on snails if the ground is dry and they can't liberate the odd worm.

The population generally moves south during the winter, with Scottish Song Thrushes coming to England and the English flocks heading as far south as Portugal. Despite an influx from Scandinavia, the UK population is declining sharply, although this is probably due to loss of habitat and nesting sites rather than increased predation from other birds.

Turdus philomelos
Length: **23cm**
Wingspan: **34cm**
Weight: **80g**
Breeding pairs: **1 million**
Present: **All year**
Status: **Red**

Starling

Starlings are mainly black with rusty-coloured legs. They tend to develop speckles during the winter, although the female has fewer. She also has a pink base to her bill, while the male's is blue. In spring, their plumage glows with a greenish iridescence. Their young are much duller brown with white speckles on the belly. They moult in the autumn and gain their adult plumage. They have angular wings and can fly extremely fast.

They breed from the middle of April. The male builds a grassy nest in a small hole in a tree or building. He may add leaves as decoration to attract a mate, but the female applies the finishing touch by lining it with feathers. She lays one or two clutches of up to nine eggs. Both parents share the job of incubating them for the next two weeks. They both feed the hatchlings with invertebrates, but they will also eat insects, worms, berries and food scraps thrown out by humans.

Their young soon leave the nest and join large flocks that include migratory birds arriving from the continent. Despite there being up to a million breeding pairs in the UK, their overall population has declined by more than 70% so they are on the red list for conservation concern. The decline is due to loss of habitat and food, and predation on their young.

Sturnus vulgaris

Length: **22cm**
Wingspan: **40cm**
Weight: **80g**
Breeding pairs: **1 million**
Present: **All year**
Status: **Red**

Swallow

Swallows are easily mistaken for House Martins, Swifts and Sand Martins but they have comparatively longer wings and tail streamers. They have metallic blue backs and wings, a cream belly, a red-brown forehead and darker collar. The female has shorter tail streamers, as do the juveniles, and the young are also without the distinctive colours on the forehead and throat.

Hirundo rustica

Length: **18cm**
Wingspan: **32cm**
Weight: **20g**
Breeding pairs: **500,000**
Present: **Summer**
Status: **Amber**

The birds arrive from South Africa in March and breed in April and May, with both parents building a muddy nest on building ledges or on cliffs. They will often renovate old nests and use them year after year. The female lays 2-3 clutches of up to eight eggs, which she alone will incubate for two weeks. Both parents feed the young with a variety of insects. They will even supply food to their young on the wing once they've fledged and flown the nest. A few birds remain in the south of England for the winter but most return to Africa.

Swift

Swifts swoop in large flocks at incredible speed. They are a dirty brown colour with a white tuft on the throat and dark bill and legs. Their tails aren't as forked as the Swallow but they look similar in flight and often catch insects and spiders on the wing. Their legs are extremely short so they can't walk or take off from the ground. In fact, other than when in the nest, they spend their entire lives in the air. As such, it's difficult to gauge population numbers but they are thought to be declining in the UK.

Apus apus

Length: **17cm**
Wingspan: **45cm**
Weight: **42g**
Breeding pairs: **75,000**
Present: **Summer**
Status: **Amber**

The breeding season begins in early summer when they arrive from Africa. They make a nest from grass and feathers in holes in walls, and the female lays a single clutch of three eggs. The parents share incubation duties for three weeks and they will both feed the young with insects caught on the wing. Juveniles spend up to eight weeks fledging before they head back to Africa in August.

Tawny Owl

Tawny Owls are widespread across England, Wales and the lowlands of Scotland, but they aren't found in Ireland. The birds are stoutly built and have brown plumage with hints of grey or red that's speckled with streaks. This allows them to blend in to the tree canopy so that they are almost invisible. Other species often disturb roosting owls to force them out of their territory.

Strix aluco

Length: **38cm**
Wingspan: **100cm**
Weight: **400g**
Breeding pairs: **20,000**
Present: **All year**
Status: **Green**

Their distinctive 'hoo-hoo-ooooo' call is a territorial call, to which another male might answer. They have many other calls that are used sparingly, however. Breeding begins in March when the female will look for a nest in a hole in a wall or tree. She incubates a single clutch of up to seven eggs for a month, although both parents will feed the chicks. They eat voles, mice, rabbits, small birds and amphibians, striking from above after stalking their prey. Juveniles fledge after another month or so and disperse to find their own territories before winter sets in.

Tree Sparrow

Tree Sparrows are slightly built and have a brown crown with a white collar and cheeks. Their backs and wings are a velvety brown and their chests and slightly paler. They have small black bills and bibs. Young birds have similar markings but they are duller in colour.

The breeding season begins in April so both parents build a twig-, moss- and hair-lined nest

Passer montanus

Length: **14cm**
Wingspan: **21cm**
Weight: **22g**
Breeding pairs: **100,000**
Present: **All year**
Status: **Red**

in a hole in a tree or wall. The female lays a couple of clutches of around six eggs but the male shares incubation duties over the next two weeks. He also helps feed the young while they fledge for another fortnight. The young leave their birthplace to find their own territories but they are unlikely to travel far. A few migratory birds will arrive in the UK for the winter but the native population has been declining rapidly for the last 20 years so they are on the red list.

Turtle Dove

Turtle Doves have bluish heads, check patches on their necks, pink chests, white bellies and chestnut brown backs and wings. The young are duller and browner. Their song sounds like the 'turr-turr' of a cat's purr.

The breeding season begins in April when the birds arrive from central Africa. They build their fragile twig nests in trees, parks and gardens and the female lays a couple of clutches of two eggs. The male shares incubation duties for the next two weeks and he also helps feed the chicks for three weeks after they've hatched. The birds eat fruit and seeds and not much else.

Four months after they arrive, the birds return to Africa for the winter. In the last half century numbers in the UK have fallen by 80% due to a loss of food and nesting sites. They are also shot for sport and food while crossing continental Europe.

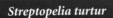

Streptopelia turtur

Length: **26cm**
Wingspan: **52cm**
Weight: **150g**
Breeding pairs: **75,000**
Present: **Summer**
Status: **Red**

Willow Tit

It's difficult to tell the Willow Tit from the Marsh Tit but the former's cap is duller, its bib is bigger and it has a pale patch on its wing. The borders between its colours are also less well defined and its short neck gives it a hunched appearance. It can also be confused with the Coal Tit and Blackcap, but the Willow Tit has a buzzing nasal call.

Poecile montanus

Length: **12cm**
Wingspan: **18cm**
Weight: **10g**
Breeding pairs: **25,000**
Present: **All year**
Status: **Red**

They breed in April and May so the female finds a hole in a tree or stump and lines it with bark and feathers. She lays a single clutch of up to 13 eggs and incubates them alone for two weeks. The male will provide food for the hatchlings and they eat a mix of insects, nuts and berries. They are also known to store food in case supplies become scarce in the winter. Willow Tits stay near their birthplace for life but their population is in serious decline due to changes in woodland management and competition with other species.

Wood Pigeon

Wood Pigeons are almost completely grey, although they have a pink tint to their chests and a green, white and purple patch on the neck. Younger birds are browner and don't have the neck patch. Europe's largest pigeon looks a little squat but its feathers fluff up to give it its plump appearance when it is actually surprisingly agile (during the mating season, males perform acrobatics to attract females).

Breeding begins in April and both sexes build a nest in a tree or on a building.

Columba palumbus

Length: **40cm**
Wingspan: **77cm**
Weight: **500g**
Breeding pairs:
2.5 million
Present: **All year**
Status: **Green**

The female lays three clutches of two eggs and both parents incubate them for the next two weeks. The young fledge for another month or so, during which time the male and female provide seeds and grains to eat. Their diet is so dry that they use their bills like straws to suck water from ponds and puddles.

Most Wood Pigeons are sedentary and rarely stray far from their roosts or feeding grounds. The UK population is boosted by Scandinavian birds passing through in winter, and their overall numbers continue to increase.

Wren

The tiny Wren only weighs about the same as a pound coin but it's a stout bird with deep brown plumage and a short but active tail. Their flanks have darker bars, but their chests are a little paler. The young are similar to the adults but they

don't develop a distinctive eyebrow until they moult. It flies in straight lines with a rapid wing-beat.

They breed in April and are happy to use nest boxes or build their own nests. The male will build a globe-shaped enclosure from grass and moss but the female will line it with feathers. She alone incubates two clutches of around six eggs for two weeks but the male will provide food in the form of spiders, insects and bugs.

British Wrens will travel to new nesting or feeding grounds when food becomes scarce. Their European neighbours often travel up to 1,500 miles to avoid the winter as the cold can decimate the population. Their numbers have been increasing in recent mild winters.

Troglodytes troglodytes

Length: **9cm**
Wingspan: **15cm**
Weight: **10g**
Breeding pairs: **7 million**
Present: **All year**
Status: **Green**

Yellow Wagtail

Yellow Wagtails arrive in the UK in spring from Sub-Saharan Africa. They have a bright yellow chest and face, olive green back and flanks, and darker wings. Females aren't as brightly coloured and have browner backs, while their young are similar albeit a little duller. Their song is a simple repetitive tweet.

Motacilla flava

Length: **15cm**
Wingspan: **25cm**
Weight: **19g**
Breeding pairs: **50,000**
Present: **Summer**
Status: **Red**

The female builds a little cup-shaped nest in a hollow on the ground. As they are vulnerable to predators, she tries to find somewhere secluded and lays a couple of clutches of five eggs. She incubates them for two weeks but the male will help feed the hatchlings while they fledge for the next two weeks. They eat the insects and beetles that accompany horses and other livestock. The birds head back south at the end of the British summer.

Yellowhammer

The Yellowhammer is largely yellow but it has browner wings with dark streaks. It also has a grey bill and chestnut rump. The female is more of a speckled and streaked brown, while juveniles are darker than their mothers.

The female builds a grassy nest in hedges or shrubs in late April. She then lays two or three clutches of up to six eggs and incubates them for

Emberiza citrinella

Length: **16cm**
Wingspan: **26cm**
Weight: **27g**
Breeding pairs: **1.2 million**
Present: **All year**
Status: **Red**

two weeks. The male will help feed the hatchlings with seed and grain.

Their numbers have declined sharply in the last quarter of a century so they are now on the red list. This is due to changes in farming restricting their food supply, although this could be addressed by managing hedgerows, field margins and crop plantation.